IF F(

👤 _____

✉ _____

📱 _____

Greater Than a Tourist Book Series
Reviews from Readers

I think the series is wonderful and beneficial for tourists to get information before visiting the city. -Seckin Zumbul, Izmir Turkey

I am a world traveler who has read many trip guides but this one really made a difference for me. I would call it a heartfelt creation of a local guide expert instead of just a guide. -Susy, Isla Holbox, Mexico

New to the area like me, this is a must have! -Joe, Bloomington, USA

This is a good series that gets down to it when looking for things to do at your destination without having to read a novel for just a few ideas. -Rachel, Monterey, USA

Good information to have to plan my trip to this destination. -Pennie Farrell, Mexico

Great ideas for a port day. -Mary Martin USA

Aptly titled, you won't just be a tourist after reading this book. You'll be greater than a tourist! -Alan Warner, Grand Rapids, USA

Even though I only have three days to spend in San Miguel in an upcoming visit, I will use the author's suggestions to guide some of my time there. An easy read - with chapters named to guide me in directions I want to go. -Robert Catapano, USA

Great insights from a local perspective! Useful information and a very good value! -Sarah, USA

This series provides an in-depth experience through the eyes of a local. Reading these series will help you to travel the city in with confidence and it'll make your journey a unique one. -Andrew Teoh, Ipoh, Malaysia

>TOURIST

GREATER THAN A TOURIST – GALVESTON TEXAS USA

50 Travel Tips from a Local

Sharon G. Walker

Greater Than a Tourist- Galveston, Texas USA Copyright © 2018 by CZYK Publishing LLC. All Rights Reserved.

All rights reserved. No part of this book may be reproduced in any form or by any electronic or mechanical means including information storage and retrieval systems, without permission in writing from the author. The only exception is by a reviewer, who may quote short excerpts in a review.

Cover designed by: Ivana Stamenkovic
Cover Image: https://pixabay.com/en/galveston-texas-moody-gardens-404510/

Greater Than a Tourist
Visit our website at www.GreaterThanaTourist.com

Lock Haven, PA
All rights reserved.
ISBN: 9781983308864

>TOURIST

50 TRAVEL TIPS FROM A LOCAL

>TOURIST

BOOK DESCRIPTION

Are you excited about planning your next trip?

Do you want to try something new?

Would you like some guidance from a local?

If you answered yes to any of these questions, then this Greater Than a Tourist book is for you.

Greater Than a Tourist- Galveston, Texas USA by Sharon G. Walker offers the inside scoop on Galveston. Most travel books tell you how to travel like a tourist. Although there is nothing wrong with that, as part of the Greater Than a Tourist series, this book will give you travel tips from someone who has lived at your next travel destination.

In these pages, you will discover advice that will help you throughout your stay. This book will not tell you exact addresses or store hours but instead will give you excitement and knowledge from a local that you may not find in other smaller print travel books.

Travel like a local. Slow down, stay in one place, and get to know the people and the culture. By the time you finish this book, you will be eager and prepared to travel to your next destination.

TABLE OF CONTENTS

BOOK DESCRIPTION
TABLE OF CONTENTS
DEDICATION
ABOUT THE AUTHOR
HOW TO USE THIS BOOK
FROM THE PUBLISHER
OUR STORY
WELCOME TO
> TOURIST
INTRODUCTION
1. Use the Airport Closest to Galveston
2. Enjoy the Ride Over the Causeway
3. Pack Plenty of Suntan Lotion
4. Enjoy a full day of fun
5. Admire the Pelican "Air Force"
6. Take the Free Ferry
7. How to Get Around
8. Get a Picture at One of the Sea Turtle Statues
9. Explore a Submarine
10. Try the "Have-a-Cow" Shake from Star Drug Store
11. Leave the Baby at Home, But Take the Baby Powder
12. Make Friends With the Wind God

13. Visit the Tall Ship "Elissa"
14. This Jelly Is Not Good On Toast
15. Take Care of Your Feet
16. Take a Party Boat Fishing Trip
17. Wet a Line at the 61st Street Pier
18. Take a Helicopter Ride
19. Parents, See One More SpongeBob Adventure
20. Welcome the Pirates With an "Ahoy, Matey"
21. Fill Your Sweet Tooth at LaKing's Confectionary
22. Walk the Seawall
23. Holiday at "Dickens on the Strand"
24. Take a Marine Biology Tour
25. See the "Tree Sculptures"
26. See the 1937 Shrimp Boat "Santa Maria"
27. Explore Broadway Cemetery
28. At the Strand and Seawall, Pay for Parking at a Pay Station
29. Get a One-Day All Water Fishing License
30. Go Shelling
31. Get the Lay of the Land
32. Have a Salt-Free Swim Experience at the Schlitterbahn.
33. Do Your Souvenir Shopping at Murdoch's
34. Yes, Go to a Library
35. Stuff in the Seafood at "Shrimp and Stuff"

>TOURIST

36. Try the Mexican Food at The Original Mexican Café
37. Try the Mexican Food at The Original Mexican Café
38. Go to Moody Gardens
39. Pick Your Beach
40. Play at Pleasure Pier
41. Carry Your Own Seating
42. Learn About the 1900 Storm
43. Walk the Strand Historic District
44. Take Sandcastle 101
45. Chill Out at "Hey,Mikey's Homemade Ice Cream Shop"
46. Come to Mardi Gras
48. Make Your First Stop the Galveston Visitors' Center
49. Have a Piece of Gaido's Pecan Pie
50. Learn to Speak Texan

TOP REASONS TO BOOK THIS TRIP

For more information, check out these websites:

50 THINGS TO KNOW ABOUT PACKING LIGHT FOR TRAVEL

Packing and Planning Tips

Travel Questions

Travel Bucket List

NOTES

DEDICATION

This book is dedicated to my parents, who worked so hard providing for our family that they did not get to travel as much as they deserved.

ABOUT THE AUTHOR

I am an enthusiastic traveler and writer who lives on the Texas Gulf Coast. I love living close to the water, where I can smell the salt in the air and hear the seagulls everywhere I go. I love standing on the beach watching a glorious sunset.

I was born and raised in Houston,Tx. As an only child, I spent a lot of time reading, writing, and studying. I got a B.A. in secondary education with minors in English and math. My first career was teaching middle school math, which I loved. While I was teaching, I got my M.Ed. in Guidance and Counseling with minors in English and math. After 8 years of teaching, I moved to College Station, Tx and earned my Ph.D. in counseling psychology. Yes, I guess all that qualifies me as a genuine nerd. I ran a private practice as a psychologist for 30 years in Houston. I am now semi-retired and work part-time providing counseling to residents of nursing homes.

I like to travel (of course), write, play No Limit Hold 'Em, work puzzles of all kinds, sit on my porch and watch it rain, and spend time with my family. My real passions are writing and teaching. I am single and live with my sweet cat, Sassy.

>TOURIST

HOW TO USE THIS BOOK

The Greater Than a Tourist book series was written by someone who has lived in an area for over three months. The goal of this book is to help travelers either dream or experience different locations by providing opinions from a local. The author has made suggestions based on their own experiences. Please do your own research before traveling to the area in case the suggested places are unavailable.

FROM THE PUBLISHER

Traveling can be one of the most important parts of a person's life. The anticipation and memories that you have are some of the best. As a publisher of the Greater Than a Tourist book series, as well as the popular 50 Things to Know book series, we strive to help you learn about new places, spark your imagination, and inspire you. Wherever you are and whatever you do I wish you safe, fun, and inspiring travel.

Lisa Rusczyk Ed. D.
CZYK Publishing

\>TOURIST

OUR STORY

Traveling is a passion of the "Greater than a Tourist" series creator. Lisa studied abroad in college, and for their honeymoon Lisa and her husband toured Europe. During her travels to Malta, an older man tried to give her some advice based on his own experience living on the island since he was a young boy. She was not sure if she should talk to the stranger but was interested in his advice. When traveling to some places she was wary to talk to locals because she was afraid that they weren't being genuine. Through her travels, Lisa learned how much locals had to share with tourists. Lisa created the "Greater Than a Tourist" book series to help connect people with locals. A topic that locals are very passionate about sharing.

>TOURIST

WELCOME TO
> TOURIST

\>TOURIST

INTRODUCTION

To travel is to take a journey into yourself." —
Danny Kaye

Galveston, Texas is a city that has re-invented itself many times because of the damage, and sometimes devastation, caused by hurricanes. She is a town that is proud of her resilience and courage in the face of extreme hardship. Each resurrection seems to bring advancement and the city just keeps getting better and better. Galvestonians are particularly passionate about their history, which traces back thousands of years.

Galveston's archeological beginnings go back to the Karankawa Indians. No one seems to know exactly where they came from, but some carbon-dated artifacts suggest that they came from the Amazon through the Caribbean to the Gulf Coast. Evidence suggests that they were in the area from the B.C.E 5th millennium (about 6,000 years ago). Battles with explorers and Texan colonists rendered them extinct as an organized tribe by 1891.

A French explorer made the first map of the island and bay area around 1721, but left the land unnamed. In 1785, a Spanish explorer named it "San Luis." The first European settlers established a settlement in 1816, led by the pirate Louis-Michel Aury. In 1817, the pirate, Jean Lafitte, took over the island and ran his smuggling operations out of the city until 1821 when the US ordered him to leave after he attacked a US vessel. Aury came back and took the reins again. In 1836, after the Texas revolution, a Canadian paid the Austin Colony $50,000 for the land on the coast and officially established Galveston.

Galveston became a center of slave trading. In 1860, census records show that one-sixth of the city's population were slaves. A Civil War battle was fought around Galveston, as Texas had joined the war on the side of the Confederacy. In 1891, embattlements were built in Galveston on the east end of the island and Fort Campbell was established. Fort Campbell was used as a POW camp during WWII. You can still see remnants of both Fort Campbell and the embattlements.

Galveston was almost destroyed by a hurricane that hit without warning in September of 1900 and created winds of up to 125 mph. An estimated 8,000-12,000 people were killed and the town was almost

>TOURIST

leveled. The incredible seawall was built during the next four years to protect the city from further storms. As you might guess, it took Galveston a while to recover.

Galveston became a tourist destination in the 1920s and 1930s. Some of the entertainment venues became businesses that interested vice detectives. The city took advantage of prohibition to bring in casinos and speak easy operations. When prohibition was repealed, Galveston tourism vanished along with it.

Galveston played a role in WWII. The Galveston Airport was taken over by the military and the Corps of Engineers built 3 runways that were 6000' in length. The Army Air Corps planes stationed there were used to patrol the Gulf for submarines. The airport is now known as Scholes Field.

As the city has continued to prosper, tourism has recovered and is now the staple of Galveston commerce. The cruise terminal is also a source for tourists and revenue as is the fishing and shrimping industry.

This book has been compiled to give the reader some insights about Galveston from a local who is passionate about the city. It is my hope that you can find things to love about my wonderful city.

What you are about to read is a collection of tips for those visiting Galveston for the first time. If you have not already seen Galveston, maybe this guide will cause you to consider a visit soon. We locals are anxious to meet you.

>TOURIST

1. USE THE AIRPORT CLOSEST TO GALVESTON

If you can, fly into Hobby Airport in Houston, which is an easy 41- mile drive from Galveston. The drive from George Bush Intercontinental Airport is a 72-mile drive which requires you to drive across all of Houston from North to South. While it is a longer trip, you can use the toll-roads and you get to see more of Houston (at least Houston from a freeway).

2. ENJOY THE RIDE OVER THE CAUSEWAY

I love driving over the causeway! It feels like I am entering a Disney-like Island Adventureland, but on a real island. As you cross over the bridge, a land of stilted houses, bayous, wetlands, and 32 miles of beaches opens up to you. So, too, does a city that has risen from the depths of destruction more than once, but has never lost its gumption.

After you cross the bridge, if you are anxious to see the gulf, take 61st St. to the right and drive until you reach Seawall Blvd. and there you are. If you want to see a bit of the city first, stay on the freeway, which will become Broadway Blvd., the main thoroughfare in town.

3. PACK PLENTY OF SUNTAN LOTION

I know. This seems like a no-brainer, but I include it because many visitors live inland in the US and have not been to the beach. I just want to remind you that beach + sun + salt + wind = serious sunburn, unless you protect yourself well. Slather on the high-grade sun screen and remember that it washes off in the surf, so re-apply it every couple of hours. It is tempting to get your tan in one day on the beach, but this is not likely to happen. What you will get if you spend all day in the sun is a painfully red skin-not tan. Your skin will blister if you linger too long. Limit your time exposed to the sun and avoid some serious pain. If you do get burned, cool it off with some

>TOURIST

vinegar. Remember to wear some head cover, too, to avoid scalp burn.

4. ENJOY A FULL DAY OF FUN

During the summer, you can play and play since the sun comes up around 6AM and fades around 8:30PM. There are plenty of things to do after dark, too, if you have any energy left. My favorite thing is to take a drink to the Seawall and watch the waves come in. At night in the summer, prepare to battle some tank-size mosquitos. If the wind is blowing hard, the mosquitos are not able to land as easily and you might avoid the bites. If you are going to be outside after dusk, use some mosquito repellant.

5. ADMIRE THE PELICAN "AIR FORCE"

One of my favorite sights is the Pelican "Air Force." Five or six of these birds will fly together in v-formation or in one line. They move along together, make a gentle turn, and glide on top of the water until one or more skims the surface to engorge some fish. On land, pelicans look awkward and some might consider them ugly, but in the air, they are grace in motion. They are also one of the "mascots" of Galveston Island, along with sea turtles. They can be anywhere, of course, but you are most likely to see them close to piers where they can rest between meals.

6. TAKE THE FREE FERRY

If you ride toward the eastern tip of the island, you will find the Bolivar Ferry, which will take you to (no surprise here) Bolivar Peninsula. The departure landing is on 2nd Street. Just follow the signs. You can walk on the ferry or drive on. On the trip across the Intercoastal Canal, you should be able to see some dolphins, which we locals never tire of spotting. You probably will want to get out of the car to catch a glimpse since they sometimes swim along beside a boat. I think they like us as much as we like them. Nice arrangement.

>TOURIST

There is not much to do on the peninsula itself, but there are many subdivisions full of houses on stilts, if this is something that interests you. Just drive four or five miles down the road, then turn around, and take the ferry back.

7. HOW TO GET AROUND

If you have your own car or a rental, you might want to drive yourself around the island, but this causes the driver to miss some of the sites and some of the island transportations are just downright fun.

Galveston presents quite a few methods of transport to see the sites.

You can take the Galveston Island Trolley, which runs two different routes. One route takes you between The Strand and the seawall. You can catch it on the seawall at 25th St. There are 2 more stops on the way to The Strand. You need to get a transfer at Seawall Blvd. and 21st to take the Seawall Loop. This loop will take you to Moody Gardens. The trolley is a great way to look over the city for the first time and get oriented. Take a piece of paper and pen with you to write down the places you want to come back to.

You can jump on and off the trolley as you wish and it only costs $1 to ride. Remember that you must have correct change to put in the fare box. The driver cannot give you change.

You can take limousines, taxis, and shuttles that different agencies run. You can find their phone numbers in most of the travel guides. You certainly want to call your hotel before you leave home to see if they have a free shuttle from the airport. If not, you can likely find some type of transportation at the airport. Bush Intercontinental Airport (IAH) is 72 miles from Galveston, making taxi fare expensive. You might want to share with another family, if possible, to cut some costs. It is a shame to spend good recreation money on transportation to the hotel. You might also be able to catch a shuttle run by a private business.

You can rent an e-bike. It is easy to get the hang of riding these small bikes and it is fun to have the wind in your face. The company that seems to be the favorite of tourists is Zipp E-bikes which is located on Mechanic Street in The Strand. They have several styles of bikes to choose from, including one with a child seat. They seem reasonably priced unless you have a large family. You already know how things add up.

>TOURIST

You can rent a regular bike. There are several companies that rent bicycles and they are located up and down the Seawall. Just about the time you cannot walk another step on the seawall, you find a bike to rent. Life is good.

You can take a Segway Tour. The Segway company has six different tours that last anywhere from one to 2.5 hours, depending on how much you want to see. I have been told that it is easy to learn to ride one, but you need to be able to stand for a while. You can rent your ride on 25th at Church St. in The Strand. If you book your reservations online, you can rent a GoPro to video your tour.

You can do the Duck Boat Tour, which is one of my favorites. A duck boat, in case you have not heard of one, is an amphibious vehicle that can maneuver on the land or on water. Being able to just drive into the water makes this a more exciting drive and it allows you to see a variety of sites. Here's a history trivia: duck boats (DUKW) were used in WWII to ferry supplies to troops after the D-Day landings.

You can take the bus. Fares are $1.05. This is probably the least expensive way to tour the city, but not very exciting.

You can take a horse-drawn carriage ride on The Strand. The strand requires abundant walking and the carriage could be a good way to see it all and mark out what attractions or shops you want to visit in person. It also gives your feet a breather.

You can take a Texas Pedal Tour that leaves out of Harbor House. This is a 1-2 hour island tour that everyone seems to enjoy. The owners of the company are very friendly and entertaining and the camaraderie of the fellow travelers is usually awesome. The way it works is that riders sit on each side of the pedal mechanism and use their feet to propel the vehicle, if they wish. All my friends and visitors who have taken the ride totally enjoyed it and could not wait to do it again.

8. GET A PICTURE AT ONE OF THE SEA TURTLE STATUES

I consider the sea turtle to be one of the mascots(symbols) of Galveston. Sea turtles have been an endangered species for a while and Galveston is proud that sea turtles picked an area on one of our beaches to nest. During hatching season, that beach is partially closed to protect their nesting grounds.

>TOURIST

There has been a project to put sculptures of them around town. Watch out for them and remember that they make a cute photo op.

9. EXPLORE A SUBMARINE

Mosey on over to Sea Wolf Park on Pelican Island and take a tour of a WWII submarine, the USS Cavalla, which is credited with sinking a Japanese aircraft carrier that attacked Pearl Harbor. Seeing the close quarters in the submarine may help you appreciate your "cramped" hotel room.

You can also take a look at the USS Stewart, a destroyer escort.

You get to Pelican Island by taking 51st Street north from the Seawall via the Pelican Island Causeway.

10. TRY THE "HAVE-A-COW" SHAKE FROM STAR DRUG STORE

Just the best there is. They come in three "colors," depending on what soft drink flavor you choose.

What everyone likes about this place is the soda fountain, which has the feel of the early 1900s. Their menu is fun with many favorites. They close the kitchen at 3PM, but from 3-4, they feature drinks, ice cream, and shopping.

11. LEAVE THE BABY AT HOME, BUT TAKE THE BABY POWDER

Okay. You can take the baby, too, if you must, but you will need the baby powder to help dislodge the sand (which will not brush off and messes up any towel you use to swipe it) from your body. Baby powder absorbs the moisture and the sand slides off easily.

12. MAKE FRIENDS WITH THE WIND GOD

While you are contemplating all the things that you will need for the beach, remember to factor in the wind, which blows constantly and sometimes very hard. It will blow away nearly everything you try to nail down to provide shade. Even those friendly looking beach umbrellas can be seen dancing down the beach with several beleaguered tourists running after them. So be prepared and take with you anything you might use to fasten your umbrella down. It is hard to shove them deep enough in to the sand to win the battle with high winds.

13. VISIT THE TALL SHIP "ELISSA"

Galveston is the proud home of the majestic 19-sail barque, the Elissa. She is one of the oldest ships sailing today. Elissa was built in Aberdeen, Scotland and launched in 1877. She sailed under the flags of Norway, Sweden and Finland as a merchant ship. She underwent several conversions by changing the sail configuration and sailed under the flag of Greece until she was bought by the San Francisco Maritime Museum in 1970. She was not refurbished for another 5 years when she was bought by the Galveston Historical Foundation.

She is currently moored at the Texas Seaport Museum close to Pier 21 and is regularly sailed by a crew of experts from all over the country. She was declared a National Historical Landmark in 1990.

The public cannot sail on the Elissa at the present time, but she is open to be toured. Step inside this sea-tossed vessel and get a feel for how the seamen lived. She can still sail you into history.

14. THIS JELLY IS NOT GOOD ON TOAST

I am talking about the jellyfish, an obnoxious, little gremlin that shares the water with us. They are sometimes called a "cabbage head" by locals because they have an almost translucent dome-shaped head. They also have fine tentacles which sting upon contact. That's the bad news. The good news is that their interference with a good day at the beach is rare. But if a sting happens, it will help if you know what to do. Remove the tentacles with tweezers or scrape off with a credit card. Rinse the sting area with vinegar for about 30 seconds. Take some ibuprofen, cover the sting area with some calamine lotion or lidocaine, and apply ice. Then you can usually ride it out and the pain will gradually diminish. Locals will tell you to use sand to get the tentacles out, but a doctor told me this was not a good plan and recommended the vinegar. Take a big jug with you. You can never be too prepared for this floating intruder.

15. TAKE CARE OF YOUR FEET

Take some good walking shoes to walk The Strand, the seawall, and Moody Gardens. Get some shoes to protect you at the beach because the SAND IS HOT. Thongs probably work best here. Some people like to get some swimming shoes that they can wear into the water easily, too.

16. TAKE A PARTY BOAT FISHING TRIP

If you want to get out on the water, consider a fishing trip on a party boat. You can fish in the bay a mile or so out or you can go deep sea fishing. You can fish for 4 hours up to 12 hours. The party boat captain will teach you how to handle the tackle, which they will provide for you. There is some question as to whether you need a fishing license. Legally, you do, but captains usually ignore this. There is no way to know if a game warden will board the boat looking for illegal fisherman or not. It does not happen often. You can obtain a one-day fishing license (see tip #29).

17. WET A LINE AT THE 61ST STREET PIER

If you want to do some fishing without going out on a boat, this is probably your best bet. The pier is off the Seawall at (you guessed it) 61st Street. It is more than just a pier. It juts out over the Gulf of Mexico and is a good place to hook trout, drum, redfish, or dolphin fish (a dolphin fish is not the dolphin we all know and love. Those are actually mammals). The dolphin fish is also called a mahi mahi and has graced many seafood feasts. The pier rents out tackle, sells bait and food, and there are always people there to help you. Check out their website to get info on prices and amenities. They are open 24/7.

18. TAKE A HELICOPTER RIDE

If you want to get a different perspective on the island, take a helicopter tour. I have never done this because I am afraid of heights, but my friends who have done it say it is worth the money and the anxiety.

You can find the helicopters at Stewart Beach on the east end of the seawall. There are seven or eight tours to choose from.

19. PARENTS, SEE ONE MORE SPONGEBOB ADVENTURE

You will find this fun voyage and the Discovery Pyramid at Moody Gardens.

Your kids will be thrilled with the interactive nature of the SpongeBob SubPants Adventure where they choose the destination and interact with silly

Captain Patrick Star. No two voyages are the same because the kids actually create the agenda. We won't tell anyone when you enjoy the ride as much as your kids do.

Discovery Pyramid has many other activities to entertain and educate both you and your children.

20. WELCOME THE PIRATES WITH AN "AHOY, MATEY"

Yes, there were pirates on the Island, most notably Jean Lafitte. Lafitte's early history is shrouded in confusion and historians debate over his birthplace and his parentage. He is believed to have started his illegal activities while still a youth when he went to work for his brother, Pierre. They set up operations on Barataria just south of New Orleans in the Mississippi River delta. Their smuggling and piracy business drew the attention of the US government and around 1814, the military made forceful entry in to Barataria Bay and captured about 80 inhabitants, some of them Lafitte's men. Late in 1814, Lafitte achieved full pardons for those arrested by making a deal with Andrew Jackson to help defend New

>TOURIST

Orleans from the British during the War of 1812. Lafitte had previously been made an offer from the British to help them against the US. He refused, thinking he could more easily deal with the US military than the British Navy if push came to shove.

He came to Galveston in 1817 to meet up with two Mexican revolutionaries, but they left soon after his arrival. Lafitte took over the island and called his pirate "kingdom" Campeche. He and his brother Pierre had a thriving smuggling business, including some dealings in slavery. They were asked to leave the Island in 1821 because they had rudely attacked some American vessels.

Lafitte continued to run his enterprises in other locales, but he is believed to have died attacking a British vessel in 1823. He was only 43. His remains can be found on Harborside St. between 14th and 15th Streets. You can see the story of this rogue and his "Campeche" at Pier21 Theatre.

21. FILL YOUR SWEET TOOTH AT LAKING'S CONFECTIONARY

LaKing's Confectionary is packed with sweet goodies like an old-time candy shop. They have candy, homemade fudge, and taffy. If you get there at the right time, you can watch someone make the taffy and then pull it. This is always fun to watch. They sell Purity Ice Cream, which they make. It has more butterfat, but is very tasty. Many locals think it is the best ice cream in the city, but it is a bit pricey. Others favor Oh, Mikey's Ice Cream Shop. (see tip #45)

22. WALK THE SEAWALL

No trip to Galveston would be complete if you did not walk down at least part of the famous Galveston Seawall.

In 1900, Galveston was virtually destroyed by a hurricane (see tip #47) that killed up to 12000 people. It also washed away hundreds of feet of beachfront. In the clean-up in the aftermath, the city decided that it had to protect the city from further damage like that and a plan was made to build a wall that could help prevent inundation by high waves, sand erosion, and flooding.

The construction began in September of 1902 and was completed in July of 1904. It was originally 2.3 miles long, but through the years has been extended to 10 miles. It is 17 feet high and 16 feet thick at the base. The wall required 11 million cubic feet of dirt and actually raised the sea level of the city by 17 feet at the seawall to about a foot at the Harbor. Back then, it cost $2.1 million to complete. Since then, it has done its job, lessening damage from many storms that Galveston has endured.

23. HOLIDAY AT "DICKENS ON THE STRAND"

If you brave the chilly wind to venture into Galveston during the Christmas season, you will be in for a real treat. "Dickens on the Strand" is a Christmas festival in the tradition of Dickens' Victorian England. Locals don period costumes and stroll the busy streets with visitors. Costumes for visitors are not required, of course, but enough people create them that The Strand, for a few days, takes on the atmosphere of a British festival. Shops and restaurants carry on the theme and some decorate with a 19th century look. You will have to check on exact dates as they change each year.

24. TAKE A MARINE BIOLOGY TOUR

At the Texas Seaport Museum on the port side of the island, you can take part in a science tour that goes out on a 60' catamaran and trawls for marine samples, including plankton and other sea life. Back on land, you get to touch the samples and look at them under a microscope. The tour only goes out about once a month and is captained by a marine biologist. The 2-hour tour embarks at Pier 21 around 10AM. You will have to contact the museum to find out the dates.

>TOURIST

25. SEE THE "TREE SCULPTURES"

In 2008, Hurricane Ike destroyed much of Galveston, including 40,000 trees. Many residents did not want to tear down what remained of their beloved trees and they left the stumps, painful reminders of the devastation. A group of artists decided to convert the ragged stumps into a reminder of a city that rose again and set about to carve the stumps into works of art. There are about 35 of them completed and more on the way.

The trees are in the historic east end, scattered over several blocks. The only tour that guides you to all of them is the Segway tour, which I highly recommend if you do not want to walk the distance. The people who run these tours will teach you to ride the Segways safely and stay nearby to help you out if need be. You can sign up for one of these guided tours at their shop in The Strand at 25th and Church Street. The tours are not cheap, but if you can stand up for the duration, you can get some great information about Galveston and see much of one neighborhood. SegCity offers 5 other group tours and private tours.

26. SEE THE 1937 SHRIMP BOAT "SANTA MARIA"

The shrimp boat Santa Maria has been part of the Galveston fleet since it was built in 1937. The years took a toll, of course, and it was dry-docked at one time before several different people worked to restore it. It is now docked at Pier 19 and, while you cannot board it, you can get a look at an authentic, vintage shrimp boat.

27. EXPLORE BROADWAY CEMETERY

If you are a history buff or a genealogist, you might enjoy a tour of the historic Galveston cemetery. Heck, you might just like looking at the sculptures and monuments and wondering about the lives of the people who lived and died so long ago. The cemetery is between 40th and 43rd Streets on Broadway. It is a quiet place that holds the voices of thousands.

>TOURIST

28. AT THE STRAND AND SEAWALL, PAY FOR PARKING AT A PAY STATION

You don't have to take your car to The Strand or the seawall, but if you do, you will pay for parking using a pay station. At The Strand, there is one of these at every intersection. At the seawall, they are positioned at intervals. The money is exchanged using paybyphone. If you plan on parking while in the city, it is a good idea to go to paybyphone.com and download the app before you leave home. You can set up an account there. When you arrive and park, open the app and follow directions. You will need to have your license plate number and the number of the area you are in, which is on the sign. There is also a phone number posted that you can call to arrange payment if you prefer. The app will ask you to estimate how long you will be there and it will signal you when your time has almost lapsed and you can extend your time using the app from wherever you are. Rates are $1 per hour up to 8 hours, which is really not too bad.

If you have any trouble, there are patrols which come by frequently and will help if you need it.

29. GET A ONE-DAY ALL WATER FISHING LICENSE

There is some debate among locals as to whether you need a fishing license if you are only going to fish one day. If you are a non-resident, you can purchase a one-day fishing license for both salt water and fresh water. Those under 17 do not need a license. You can usually purchase these at tackle shops or some grocery stores. In Galveston, these licenses can be purchased at Academy Sports and Wal-Mart. They currently run about $20.

30. GO SHELLING

One of my favorite things to do when I am at any beach is to look for seashells. Galveston beaches hold many varieties of shells. The major challenge in shell hunting is to find shells that are whole. It is fun to experience the sense of accomplishment when you find an undamaged one. You must know a few things to achieve this goal. One is that the best time to find them whole is right after a high wave event or a rainstorm. The second is that you have the best chance in the morning after a storm, before the beachgoers have picked the beach clean.

31. GET THE LAY OF THE LAND

Galveston is an island, elongated, and looks like a hammerhead shark eating a baseball. Okay. Rorschach test. You look at it and tell me what it looks like to you.

There are three main roads that run the length of the island going east to west. Seawall Blvd. is the southernmost road and runs almost all the way from end to end. This is the ocean side of the island(hence the name "seawall").

The central street is Broadway Street which is the main artery to get to the different regions of the city.

The northernmost street is Harborside St. which traverses most of the north side of the island. If you get lost and you find one of these streets, at least you know you are going either east or west. Most of the streets running north and south are numbered, i.e. 1st St., 2nd St., etc. or with letters of the alphabet.

32. HAVE A SALT-FREE SWIM EXPERIENCE AT THE SCHLITTERBAHN.

You may have one of these water parks close to where you live, so I would not use my Galveston time doing this; but, if you do not have one nearby, then this may be a must-do for you. Schlitterbahn is one of the best water parks anywhere and while the Galveston beaches are free, you cannot get 35 different water attractions at the beach. There are activities here for all ages, including beaches, tube riding, and the awesome Massiv, the industry's longest water slide. I like the Massiv because you ride in a vehicle (boat, tube, or raft) and it is covered at some of the scariest parts. The ride is 926 feet long and 81 feet high at its tallest. But, beware. Even the climb up to the takeoff area will scare you if you are afraid of heights. My friends literally had to get me up the stairs with my eyes closed and then quickly into a vehicle. The ride was not so scary, but there were moments where the ground was clearly a long way down. The other exciting thing about this water slide adventure is that the water pushes you up at times. This is a strange sensation. If the beach turns out to not be your thing, Schlitterbahn might be a good option for you.

33. DO YOUR SOUVENIR SHOPPING AT MURDOCH'S

If you didn't have much luck shelling, you can always go to a souvenir shop and buy some shells. Rub them in the sand and sit them in the sea water for a little bit, and who will know the difference. Then you get to make up a wild story of "recovery."

Murdoch's is located at 2215 Seawall Blvd. and is built over the water. It has been there over 50 years and has been destroyed by several hurricanes, but it has always risen again. Shopping there has been a tradition for Galvestonians for several generations.

This family shop is a great place to buy shells and thousands of other island souvenirs. Prices are very reasonable and staff is friendly and helpful. This is the place where locals take their visitors to shop.

34. YES, GO TO A LIBRARY

The Rosenberg Library was originally built in 1872 and is considered by some to be the oldest continually operating library in the US. Some think the oldest one is in Lockhart, Tx, but we never add that to our commentary. The architecture is stunning. What I like best are the exhibits that are placed on the fourth floor. They are changed out every so often and include art exhibits, historical exhibits, and just- for-fun exhibits. Take the awesome stairs if you can.

35. STUFF IN THE SEAFOOD AT "SHRIMP AND STUFF"

Galveston's best kept secret is the locals' favorite seafood place. "Shrimp and Stuff's" original restaurant is located at Ave O and 39th St. This place looks like what a seafood restaurant should look like. An old, worn building that looks like the years of sea and salt have taken a toll on it. But, inside is Galveston's best seafood. The locals are not happy that it was awarded Best Seafood in Galveston in 2017. "Now tourists will want to eat here."

>TOURIST

36. TRY THE MEXICAN FOOD AT THE ORIGINAL MEXICAN CAFÉ

If you came to Texas and you want to get some great Mexican food, check out the Original Mexican Café at the corner of Market St. and 14th, within walking distance of The Strand. This café was built in 1916, making it the oldest continuing restaurant in Galveston. It was named best margaritas in 2012 and best seafood 2013-2017.

37. TRY THE MEXICAN FOOD AT THE ORIGINAL MEXICAN CAFÉ

Galveston has a rich history, but many of its structures have been destroyed by storms. One of the places that has managed to survive even the 1900 storm is the Bishop's Palace.

This Victorian Era home was built between 1887-1892 for Colonel Grisham, a Civil War soldier. It covers about 19,000 square feet. The Catholic

Church later bought it to serve as an office and home for the then Bishop. When those offices were moved out, the residence was opened for the public.

This elegant Victorian residence is a US Registered Historical Landmark and has been described as one of the best examples of Victorian architecture in the US. It is a must see!

38. GO TO MOODY GARDENS

Moody Gardens is an adventure park located a bit out of town on the West End next to Scholes Airport. You can get drive over in your car or take the Seawall Loop on the trolley. You will be able to recognize the park from a distance by the three glass covered pyramids jutting up over the tree line. The park includes the Rainforest Pyramid, Aquarium Pyramid, and Discovery Pyramid. The latter emphasizes activities for kids. All three venues are outstanding and the setting itself is lush and inviting.

Remember if you go to the Rainforest that it will be hot and humid. Prepare to perspire (we could say that about most of summertime Galveston, but the

>TOURIST

breeze outside helps mitigate the discomfort) and carry some water. You really do not want to cut your visit to this extraordinary experience short because you get overheated.

The aquarium is home to many species native to the Gulf. It is a challenge to find them all, but a good learning experience. See if you can locate all the fish identified on the aquarium's exhibits and signage.

39. PICK YOUR BEACH

Galveston has 32 miles of sand and beach.

There are beaches along the Seawall and you can choose the one that looks best to you. Don't expect white sand, but do expect some seaweed that has been pushed in by tides. It is smelly, but you can usually find some beach that does not have any.

Aside from seawall beaches, there are others scattered around the island. Surfside Beach is down the west end of the island, past the end of the seawall, which makes it geography a bit different. Pocket Park 1 is located close to Moody Gardens. Follow Seawall Blvd. until it turns into Termini-San Luis Pass road and the beach is on this road. Pocket Park 2 is also on this road and features a wetlands preserve. Pocket Park 2 has a rinse-off shower and restrooms. Visitors are not able to go onto the dunes at either park, but they are beautiful to see. Pets are allowed at both, but owner clean-up is requested. There is some good surf fishing further down at San Luis Pass.

Stewart Beach is on the east end of the Island down Seawall Blvd. It is considered the "family" beach, partly because no alcohol is allowed. No glass bottles are allowed either. Pets are allowed on leashes and owners are expected to clean up after their pet, but many do not, making "dodge poop" a necessary game at times. Amenities abound, though, and a family can still have a good beach experience here. It was recently voted one of the top 10 family beaches in the country.

East Beach is just a little east of Stewart Beach and has the reputation of being the "party" beach. Alcohol is allowed on East Beach and it is has a pavilion and boardwalk where festivals and live concerts are held. Amazingly, there is a bird sanctuary on "partying" East Beach. I guess the birds like the music.

For those who are looking for a more sedate beach experience, the area most overlooked by tourists is actually my favorite. It is the Galveston Island State

Park beach. In 2013, the Travel Channel named this beach one of the top 5 "Best Gulf Coast Beaches." The park features a barrier island ecosystem and several different coastal terrains and is a good place to view and photograph wildlife. There is also beach for surf fishing.

The park is located on the west end of the Seawall.

40. PLAY AT PLEASURE PIER

One of the newest attractions and one that has caused a great deal of excitement is Pleasure Pier. There has been a Pleasure Pier over the water for decades in Galveston, but due to storms through the years, it has had several resurrections. The original one was destroyed in Hurricane Carla in 1961. My family remembers that hurricane. My family had hand built a small bay house in San Leon, Tx and flood waters rose from Dickinson, south of San Leon, and put a thick, layer of silt and 5 feet water in the house. The house sat on blocks and it floated off square about 20 degrees. My family was able to clean up the mess and used the house another 20 years.

Hurricane Ike in 2008 destroyed the previous Pleasure Pier and it was recently rebuilt by the Fertitta group, who own many Galveston area enterprises.

Pleasure Pier features rides, shops, and food. The ride pass seems a bit expensive, but the kids seem to love the rides and there are a few to challenge the older crowd, too, like the roller coaster. There is also a 5D theatre, which has sensory special effects, like shaking seats. The Shark Attack feature may scare small children. You can see details and pictures of the Pier at their website, pleasurepier.com

41. CARRY YOUR OWN SEATING

There can be major walking if you want to walk the Seawall or The Strand. If this will be hard for you, you might want to take along your own portable seating to allow you to sit down anywhere without having to walk blocks to find a bench. I am thinking of a camping stool or a full, aluminum folding chair, if you wish. The camping stool folds and some kinds have a cloth case with a strap for easy carrying. I have one that I bought on Amazon that is a little

>TOURIST

sturdier than a camping stool. It is made of tough plastic and has a hole that creates a handle. You could rig up a strap for easy transport. I know this may sound extreme, but having your "quick seat" available may save you from having to give up your plans when your back hurts or your feet get too tired. Just plop down, grab a drink or ice cream and watch the world go by for a time while you let your body recover.

42. LEARN ABOUT THE 1900 STORM

On September 8, 1900, Galveston was destroyed by a mighty hurricane that came in with no warning. Galveston was a town of 40,000 with a booming economy, but the city was just about leveled. Eight to twelve thousand people were killed, making it the deadliest natural disaster in the history of the US. You can see a movie about it at Pier 21 Theatre. The seawall was constructed after this storm to protect the city from flooding and erosion.

43. WALK THE STRAND HISTORIC DISTRICT

Put on your best walking shoes and head for downtown to explore The Strand. The Strand encompasses an area of 12 square blocks and is a wonderland of shops, restaurants, bars, and other attractions.

It is also the scene of the Mardi Gras festival in March and the Dickens on The Strand event around Christmastime. While the Strand is known for its shops and entertainment venues, you should pay attention to the architecture, too. Some of the buildings survived the 1900 storm and have a plaque mounted to commemorate this achievement.

44. TAKE SANDCASTLE 101

Everyone wants to build a sandcastle. How about some lessons?

The first time I took the lessons and built a sandcastle, it fell down several times and wound up in a heap, but my constructions have improved through

the years. I said "improved." I did not ⌐
have gotten "good."

Galveston's Sandcastle Days event will feature an instructor who will build a castle in the morning and then offer free lessons in the afternoon. Needed supplies will be provided on a limited basis so you should probably take your own sand bucket and shovel. You can buy these at many venues on the Seawall. This event happens at Stewart Beach Pavilion at 201 Seawall Blvd. every Saturday.

45. CHILL OUT AT "HEY,MIKEY'S HOMEMADE ICE CREAM SHOP"

Ask locals who has the best ice cream in town and they will say, "Hey Mikey's." LaKing's Confectionary has good ice cream too, but many locals prefer Mikey's. It is homemade and comes in 130 flavors, rotated through 20 at a time. Mikey's is also home to Nacho Ice Cream. Mikey's is located on Post Office Street.

46. COME TO MARDI GRAS

Two weeks before Ash Wednesday, Galveston puts on one of its best festivals, Mardi Gras. It is held on The Strand and is reminiscent of the New Orleans Mardi Gras, but not as big. There are beads galore and anything goes during these three days. The "greatest party in the world" leaves everyone smiling.

47. Experience Ultimate Show at Pier 21 Theater

Pier 21 Theater is the home to stories of Galveston's history. They change a few times a year. There is always one on the 1900 storm that devastated the island, and this is a must see, particularly if you want to understand the city's pride in its history. Galveston is the phoenix that has risen from the debris—over and over.

>TOURIST

48. MAKE YOUR FIRST STOP THE GALVESTON VISITORS' CENTER

For information on just about everything Galveston, stop by the Galveston Visitors' Center. It is on Broadway at 23rd Street at Ashton Villa. Watch closely or you will miss it since it faces north and you will probably be driving north from Broadway. At the visitors' center you will find brochures, pamphlets, and magazines devoted to Galveston and its attractions. If you contact them before your trip, they will send you a visitor's packet. There are some local volunteers there that have a lifetime of information, too.

Make sure you pick up a copy of the Island Guide and the Houston Chronicle's insert, "Galveston." These will give you detailed information about what is going on in Galveston. The Island Guide has particularly extensive data about music venues and bars, including who is appearing, to help you plan some night life adventures. They also feature articles, food guides, and fun maps of the city with attractions identified.

49. HAVE A PIECE OF GAIDO'S PECAN PIE

Gaido's is considered by some people to have the best seafood in Galveston, but it is a bit pricey. You may decide not to have a complete meal, but you must treat yourself to some pecan pie. Pecan (Puh-Con) pie must be the official state pie of Texas. Our pecans are some of the best in the world. At Gaido's, you can buy a whole pie to go or sit down and have a piece of pie and coffee. Locals say that this pie "is to die for."

50. LEARN TO SPEAK TEXAN

Ain't--- "Am not" or "Are not" or "Is not"

Some people consider this to be subpar grammar, but in Texas that ain't necessarily so. The word (if you can call it a word) makes the hair stand up on some people's neck, but when that neck is only slightly red, ain't is acceptable. Even my spell checker is trying to get me to correct "ain't" while I write this sentence.

>TOURIST

All get out: to the extreme, highest level "He got angry as all get out."

Come hell or high water: No matter what happens
"I am going to go fishing Friday night, come hell or high water."

Coke: any soft drink "Do you have Coke here? OK. Let me

have a Diet Pepsi, please."

Dang: substitute for "damn" when your mother or Sunday School teacher is around "I hit my dang finger."

Fixin' to ---getting ready to "I'm fixin' to leave."

A fixin' to---same as above "I'm a fixin' to leave."

Gonna-- going to "I'm gonna work late."

Hissy fit—a tantrum " He had a hissy fit when he heard that."

Howdy—hello   "Howdy, ya'll."

Sure 'nuff---- sure enough   " He sure 'nuff did do it."

'Til the cows come home--- a long time   "He will be paying for that until the cows come home."

>TOURIST

TOP REASONS TO BOOK THIS TRIP

1) **Entertainment**- Galveston offers tours, events, rides, displays, restaurants, shops, and water sports that can engage a visitor on many different levels.

2) **Food** ---Galveston features some of the best food in the country, particularly seafood, along with beer breweries, bars, and food shops

3) **History**- Galveston is proud of its history that dates back to Native Americans some 6000 years ago. History is highlighted by numerous shows, displays, and tours

FOR MORE INFORMATION, CHECK OUT THESE WEBSITES:

https://www.galveston.com/
https://www.galveston.com/visitorscenter/

>TOURIST

BONUS BOOK

50 THINGS TO KNOW ABOUT PACKING LIGHT FOR TRAVEL

PACK THE RIGHT WAY EVERY TIME

AUTHOR: MANIDIPA BHATTACHARYYA

First Published in 2015 by Dr. Lisa Rusczyk. Copyright 2015. All Rights Reserved. No part of this publication may be reproduced, including scanning and photocopying, or distributed in any form or by any means, electronic or mechanical, or stored in a database or retrieval system without prior written permission from the publisher.

Disclaimer: The publisher has put forth an effort in preparing and arranging this book. The information provided herein by the author is provided "as is". Use this information at your own risk. The publisher is not a licensed doctor. Consult your doctor before engaging in any medical activities. The publisher and author disclaim any liabilities for any loss of profit or commercial or personal damages resulting from the information contained in this book.

Edited by Melanie Howthorne

ABOUT THE AUTHOR

Manidipa Bhattacharyya is a creative writer and editor, with an education in English literature and Linguistics. After working in the IT industry for seven long years she decided to call it quits and follow her heart instead. Manidipa has been ghost writing, editing, proof reading and doing secondary research services for many story tellers and article writers for about three years. She stays in Kolkata, India with her husband and a busy two year old. In her own time Manidipa enjoys travelling, photography and writing flash fiction.

Manidipa believes in travelling light and never carries anything that she couldn't haul herself on a trip. However, travelling with her child changed the scenario. She seemed to carry the entire world with her for the baby on the first two trips. But good sense prevailed and she is again working her way to becoming a light traveler, this time with a kid.

INTRODUCTION

He who would travel happily
must travel light.

-Antoine de Saint-Exupéry

Travel takes you to different places from seas and mountains to deserts and much more. In your travels you get to interact with different people and their cultures. You will, however, enjoy the sights and interact positively with these new people even more, if you are travelling light.

When you travel light your mind can be free from worry about your belongings. You do not have to spend precious vacation time waiting for your luggage to arrive after a long flight. There is be no chance of your bags going missing and the best part is that you need not pay a fee for checked baggage.

People who have mastered this art of packing light will root for you to take only one carry-on, wherever you go. However, many people can find it really hard to pack light. More so if you are travelling with children. Differentiating between "must have" and "just in case" items is the starting point. There will be ample shopping avenues at your destination which are just waiting to be explored.

This book will show you 'packing' in a new 'light' – pun intended – and help you to embrace light packing practices for all of your future travels.

Off to packing!

DEDICATION

I dedicate this book to all the travel buffs that I know, who have given me great insights into the contents of their backpacks.

THE RIGHT TRAVEL GEAR

1. CHOOSE YOUR TRAVEL GEAR CAREFULLY

While selecting your travel gear, pick items that are light weight, durable and most importantly, easy to carry. There are cases with wheels so you can drag them along – these are usually on the heavy side because of the trolley. Alternatively a backpack that you can carry comfortably on your back, or even a duffel bag that you can carry easily by hand or sling across your body are also great options. Whatever you choose, one thing to keep in mind is that the luggage itself should not weigh a ton, this will give you the flexibility to bring along one extra pair of shoes if you so desire.

>TOURIST

2. CARRY THE MINIMUM NUMBER OF BAGS

Selecting light weight luggage is not everything. You need to restrict the number of bags you carry as well. One carry-on size bag is ideal for light travel. Most carriers allow one cabin baggage plus one purse, handbag or camera bag as long as it slides under the seat in front. So technically, you can carry two items of luggage without checking them in.

3. PACK ONE EXTRA BAG

Always pack one extra empty bag along with your essential items. This could be a very light weight duffel bag or even a sturdy tote bag which takes up minimal space. In the event that you end up buying a lot of souvenirs, you already have a handy bag to stuff all that into and do not have to spend time hunting for an appropriate bag.

> *I'm very strict with my packing and have everything in its right place. I never change a rule. I hardly use anything in the hotel room. I wheel my own wardrobe in and that's it.*
>
> Charlie Watts

CLOTHES & ACCESSORIES

4. PLAN AHEAD

Figure out in advance what you plan to do on your trip. That will help you to pick that one dress you need for the occasion. If you are going to attend a wedding then you have to carry formal wear. If not, you can ditch the gown for something lighter that will be comfortable during long walks or on the beach.

5. WEAR THAT JACKET

Remember that wearing items will not add extra luggage for your air travel. So wear that bulky jacket that you plan to carry for your trip. This saves space and can also help keep you warm during the chilly flight.

6. MIX AND MATCH

Carry clothes that can be interchangeably used to reinvent your look. Find one top that goes well with a couple of pairs of pants or skirts. Use tops, shirts and jackets wisely along with other accessories like a scarf or a stole to create a new look.

7. CHOOSE YOUR FABRIC WISELY

Stuffing clothes in cramped bags definitely takes its toll which results in wrinkles. It is best to carry wrinkle free, synthetic clothes or merino tops. This will eliminate the need for that small iron you usually bring along.

8. DITCH CLOTHES PACK UNDERWEAR

Pack more underwear and socks. These are the things that will give you a fresh feel even if you do not get a chance to wear fresh clothes. Moreover these are easy to wash and can be dried inside the hotel room itself.

9. CHOOSE DARK OVER LIGHT

While picking your clothes choose dark coloured ones. They are easy to colour coordinate and can last longer before needing a wash. Accidental food spills and dirt from the road are less visible on darker clothes.

10. WEAR YOUR JEANS

Take only one pair of Jeans with you, which you should wear on the flight. Remember to pick a pair that can be worn for sightseeing trips and is equally eloquent for dinner. You can add variety by adding light weight cargoes and chinos.

11. CARRY SMART ACCESSORIES

The right accessory can give you a fresh look even with the same old dress. An intelligent neck-piece, a couple of bright scarves, stoles or a sarong can be used in a number of ways to add variety to your clothing. These light weight beauties can double up as a nursing cover, a light blanket, beach wear, a modesty cover for visiting places of worship, and also makes for an enthralling game of peek-a-boo.

12. LEARN TO FOLD YOUR GARMENTS

Seasoned travellers all swear by rolling their clothes for compact and wrinkle free packing. Bundle packing, where you roll the clothes around a central object as if tying it up, is also a popular method of compact and wrinkle free packing. Stacking folded clothes one on top of another is a big no-no as it makes creases extreme and they are difficult to get rid of without ironing.

13. WASH YOUR DIRTY LAUNDRY

>TOURIST

One of the ways to avoid carrying loads of clothes is to wash the clothes you carry. At some places you might get to use the laundry services or a Laundromat but if you are in a pinch, best solution is to wash them yourself. If that is the plan then carrying quick drying clothes is highly recommended, which most often also happen to be the wrinkle free variety.

14. LEAVE THOSE TOWELS BEHIND

Regular towels take up a lot of space, are heavy and take ages to dry out. If you are staying at hotels they will provide you with towels anyway. If you are travelling to a remote place, where the availability of towels look doubtful, carry a light weight travel towel of viscose material to do the job.

15. USE A COMPRESSION BAG

Compression bags are getting lots of recommendation now days from regular travellers. These are useful for saving space in your luggage when you have to pack bulky dresses. While packing for the return trip, get help from the hotel staff to arrange a vacuum cleaner.

FOOTWEAR

16. PUT ON YOUR HIKING BOOTS

If you have plans to go hiking or trekking during your trip, you will need those bulky hiking boots. The best way to carry them is to wear them on flight to save space and luggage weight. You can remove the boots once inside and be comfortable in your socks.

17. PICKING THE RIGHT SHOES

Shoes are often the bulkiest items, along with being the dainty if you are a female. They need care and take up a lot of space in your luggage. It is advisable therefore to pick shoes very carefully. If you plan to do a lot of walking and site seeing, then wearing a pair of comfortable walking shoes are a must. For more formal occasions you can carry durable, light weight flats which will not take up much space.

18. STUFF SHOES

If you happen to pack a pair of shoes, ensure you utilize their hollow insides. Tuck small items like rolled up socks or belts to save space. They will also be easy to find.

>TOURIST

TOILETRIES

19. STASHING TOILETRIES

Carry only absolute necessities. Airline rules dictate that for one carry-on bag, liquids and gels must be in 3.4 ounce (100ml) bottles or less, and must be packed in a one quart zip-lock bag. If you are planning to stay in a hotel, the basic things will be provided for you. It's best is to buy the rest from the local market at your destination.

20. TAKE ALONG TAMPONS

Tampons are a hard to find item in a lot of countries. Figure out how many you need and pack accordingly. For longer stays you can buy them online and have them delivered to where you are staying.

21. GET PAMPERED BEFORE YOU TRAVEL

Some avid travellers suggest getting a pedicure and manicure just the day before travelling. This not only gives you a well kept look, you also save the trouble of packing nail polish. Remember, every little bit of weight reduced adds up.

ELECTRONICS
22. LUGGING ALONG ELECTRONICS

Electronics have a large role to play in our lives today. Most of us cannot imagine our lives away from our phones, laptops or tablets. However while travelling, one must consider the amount of weight these electronics add to our luggage. Thankfully smart phones come along with all the essentials tools like a camera, email access, picture editing tools and more. They are smart to the point of eliminating the need to carry multiple gadgets. Choose a smart phone that suits all your requirements and travel with the world in your palms or pocket.

23. REDUCE THE NUMBER OF CHARGERS

If you do travel with multiple electronic devices, you will have to bear the additional burden of carrying all their chargers too. Check if a single charger can be used for multiple devices. You might also consider investing in a pocket charger. These small devices support multiple devices while keeping you charged on the go.

>TOURIST

24. TRAVEL FRIENDLY APPS

Along with smart phones come numerous apps, which are immensely helpful in our travels. You name it and you have an app for it at hand – take pictures, sharing with friends and family, torch to light dark roads, maps, checking flight/train times, find hotels and many other things. Use these smart alternatives to traditional items like books to eliminate weight and save space.

I get ideas about what's essential when packing my suitcase.

-Diane von Furstenberg

TRAVELLING WITH KIDS

25. BRING ALONG THE STROLLER

Kids might enjoy walking for a while but they soon tire out and a stroller is the just the right thing for them to rest in while you continue your tour. Strollers also double duty as a luggage carrier and shopping bag holder. Remember to pick a light weight, easy to handle brand of stroller. Better yet, find out in advance if you can rent a stroller at your destination.

26. BRING ONLY ENOUGH DIAPERS FOR YOUR TRIP

Diapers take up a lot of space and add to the weight of your luggage. Therefore it is advisable to carry just enough diapers to last through the trip and a few for afterwards, till you buy fresh stock at your destination. Unless of course you are travelling to a really remote area, in which case you have no choice but to carry the load. Otherwise diapers are something you will find pretty easily.

27. TAKE ONLY A COUPLE OF TOYS

Children are easily attracted by new things in their environment. While travelling they will find numerous 'new' objects to scrutinize and play with. Packing just one favorite toy is enough, or if there is no favorite toy leave out all of them in favor of stories or imaginary games.

28. CARRY KID FRIENDLY SNACKS

Create a small snack counter in your bag to store away quick bites for those sudden hunger pangs. Depending on the child's age this could include chocolates, raisins, dry fruits, granola bars or biscuits. Also keep a bottle of water handy for your little one.

>TOURIST

These things do not add much weight and can be adjusted in a handbag or knapsack.

29. GAMES TO CARRY

Create some travel specific, imaginary games if you have slightly grown up children, like spot the attractions. Keep a coloring book and colors handy for in-flight or hotel time. Apps on your smart phone can keep the children engaged with cartoons and story books. Older children are often entertained by games available on phones or tablets. This cuts the weight of luggage down while keeping the kids entertained.

30. LET THE KIDS CARRY THEIR LOAD

A good thing is to start early sharing of responsibilities. Let your child pick a bag of his or her choice and pack it themselves. Keep tabs on what they are stuffing in their bags by asking if they will be using that item on the trip. It could start out being just an entertainment bag initially but with growing years they will learn to sort the useful from the superfluous. Children as little as four can maneuver a small trolley suitcase like a pro- their experience in pull along toys credit. If you are worried that you may be pulling it for them, you may want to start with a backpack.

31. DECIDE ON LOCATION FOR CHILDREN TO SLEEP

While on a trip you might not always get a crib at your destination, and carrying one will make life all the more difficult. Instead call ahead to see if there are any cribs or roll out beds for children. You may even put blankets on the floor. Weave them a story about camping and they will gladly sleep without any trouble.

32. GET BABY PRODUCTS DELIVERED AT YOUR DESTINATION

If you are absolutely paranoid about not getting your favourite variety of diaper or brand of baby food, check out online stores like amazon.com for services in your destination city. You can buy things online ahead of your travel and get them delivered to your hotel upon arrival.

33. FEEDING NEEDS OF YOUR INFANTS

If you are travelling with a breastfed infant, you save the trouble of carrying bottles and bottle sanitization kits. For special food, or medications, you may need

>TOURIST

to call ahead to make sure you have a refrigerator where you are staying.

34. FEEDING NEEDS OF YOUR TODDLER

With the progression from infancy to toddler, their dietary requirements too evolve. You will have to pack some snacks for travelling time. Fresh fruits and vegetables can be purchased at your destination. Most of the cities you travel to in whichever part of the world, will have baby food products and formulas, available at the local drug-store or the supermarket.

35. PICKING CLOTHES FOR YOUR BABY

Contrary to popular belief, babies can do without many changes of clothes. At the most pack 2 outfits per day. Pack mix and match type clothes for your little one as well. Pick things which are comfortable to wear and quick to dry.

36. SELECTING SHOES FOR YOUR BABY

Like outfits, kids can make do with two pairs of comfortable shoes. If you can get some water resistant shoes it will be best. To expedite drying wet shoes, you can stuff newspaper in them then wrap them with newspaper and leave them to dry overnight.

37. KEEP ONE CHANGE OF CLOTHES HANDY

Travelling with kids can be tricky. Keep a change of clothes for the kids and mum handy in your purse or tote bag. This takes a bit of space in your hand luggage but comes extremely handy in case there are any accidents or spills.

38. LEAVE BEHIND BABY ACCESSORIES

Baby accessories like their bed, bath tub, car seat, crib etc. should be left at home. Many hotels provide a crib on request, while car seats can be borrowed from friends or rented. Babies can be given a bath in the hotel sink or even in the adult bath tub with a little bit of water. If you bring a few bath toys, they can be used in the bath, pool, and out of water. They can also be sanitized easily in the sink.

39. CARRY A SMALL LOAD OF PLASTIC BAGS

With children around there are chances of a number of soiled clothes and diapers. These plastic bags help to sort the dirt from the clean inside your big bag.

>TOURIST

These are very light weight and come in handy to other carry stuff as well at times.

PACK WITH A PURPOSE

40. PACKING FOR BUSINESS TRIPS

One neutral-colored suit should suffice. It can be paired with different shirts, ties and accessories for different occasions. One pair of black suit pants could be worn with a matching jacket for the office or with a snazzy top for dinner.

41. PACKING FOR A CRUISE

Most cruises have formal dinners, and that formal dress usually takes up a lot of space. However you might find a tuxedo to rent. For women, a short black dress with multiple accessory options will do the trick.

42. PACKING FOR A LONG TRIP OVER DIFFERENT CLIMATES

The secret packing mantra for travel over multiple climates is layering. Layering traps air around your body creating insulation against the cold. The same light t-shirt that is comfortable in a warmer climate can be the innermost layer in a colder climate.

REDUCE SOME MORE WEIGHT

43. LEAVE PRECIOUS THINGS AT HOME

Things that you would hate to lose or get damaged leave them at home. Precious jewelry, expensive gadgets or dresses, could be anything. You will not require these on your trip. Leave them at home and spare the load on your mind.

44. SEND SOUVENIRS BY MAIL

If you have spent all your money on purchasing souvenirs, carrying them back in the same bag that you brought along would be difficult. Either pack everything in another bag and check it in the airport or get everything shipped to your home. Use an international carrier for a secure transit, but this could be more expensive than the checking fees at the airport.

45. AVOID CARRYING BOOKS

Books equal to weight. There are many reading apps which you can download on your smart phone or tab.

Plus there are gadgets like Kindle and Nook that are thinner and lighter alternatives to your regular book.

CHECK, GET, SET, CHECK AGAIN

46. STRATEGIZE BEFORE PACKING

Create a travel list and prepare all that you think you need to carry along. Keep everything on your bed or floor before packing and then think through once again – do I really need that? Any item that meets this question can be avoided. Remove whatever you don't really need and pack the rest.

47. TEST YOUR LUGGAGE

Once you have fully packed for the trip take a test trip with your luggage. Take your bags and go to town for window shopping for an hour. If you enjoy your hour long trip it is good to go, if not, go home and reduce the load some more. Repeat this test till you hit the right weight.

48. ADD A ROLL OF DUCT TAPE

You might wonder why, when this book has been talking about reducing stuff, we're suddenly asking you to pack something totally unusual. This is because when you have limited supplies, duct tape is immensely helpful for small repairs – a broken bag, leaking zip-lock bag, broken sunglasses, you name it and duct tape can fix it, temporarily.

49. LIST OF ESSENTIAL ITEMS

Even though the emphasis is on packing light, there are things which have to be carried for any trip. Here is our list of essentials:

- Passport/Visa or any other ID

- Any other paper work that might be required on a trip like permits, hotel reservation confirmations etc.

- Medicines – all your prescription medicines and emergency kit, especially if you are travelling with children

- Medical or vaccination records

- Money in foreign currency if travelling to a different country

- Tickets- Email or Message them to your phone

50. MAKE THE MOST OF YOUR TRIP

>TOURIST

Wherever you are going, whatever you hope to do we encourage you to embrace it whole-heartedly. Take in the scenery, the culture and above all, enjoy your time away from home.

> *On a long journey even a straw*
> *weighs heavy.*

-Spanish Proverb

>TOURIST

PACKING AND PLANNING TIPS

A Week before Leaving

- Arrange for someone to take care of pets and water plants
- Stop mail and newspaper
- Notify Credit Card companies where you are going.
- Change your thermostat settings
- Car inspected, oil is changed, and tires have the correct pressure.
- Passports and id is up to date.
- Pay bills.
- Copy important items and download travel Apps.
- Start collecting small bills for tips

Right Before Leaving

- Clean out refrigerator.
- Empty garbage cans.
- Lock windows.
- Make sure you have the right ID with you.
- Bring cash for tips.
- Remember travel documents.
- Lock door behind you.
- Remember wallet.
- Unplug items in house and pack chargers.

>TOURIST

READ OTHER GREATER THAN A TOURIST BOOKS

Greater Than a Tourist San Miguel de Allende Guanajuato Mexico: 50 Travel Tips from a Local by Tom Peterson

Greater Than a Tourist – Lake George Area New York USA: 50 Travel Tips from a Local by Janine Hirschklau

Greater Than a Tourist – Monterey California United States: 50 Travel Tips from a Local by Katie Begley

Greater Than a Tourist – Chanai Crete Greece: 50 Travel Tips from a Local by Dimitra Papagrigoraki

Greater Than a Tourist – The Garden Route Western Cape Province South Africa: 50 Travel Tips from a Local by Li-Anne McGregor van Aardt

Greater Than a Tourist – Sevilla Andalusia Spain: 50 Travel Tips from a Local by Gabi Gazon

Greater Than a Tourist – Kota Bharu Kelantan Malaysia: 50 Travel Tips from a Local by Aditi Shukla

Children's Book: Charlie the Cavalier Travels the World by Lisa Rusczyk

\>TOURIST

> TOURIST

Visit Greater Than a Tourist for Free Travel Tips
http://GreaterThanATourist.com

Sign up for the Greater Than a Tourist Newsletter for discount days, new books, and travel information:
http://eepurl.com/cxspyf

Follow us on Facebook for tips, images, and ideas:
https://www.facebook.com/GreaterThanATourist

Follow us on Pinterest for travel tips and ideas:
http://pinterest.com/GreaterThanATourist

Follow us on Instagram for beautiful travel images:
http://Instagram.com/GreaterThanATourist

>TOURIST

> TOURIST

    Please leave your honest review of this book on Amazon and Goodreads. Please send your feedback to GreaterThanaTourist@gmail.com as we continue to improve the series. Thank you. We appreciate your positive and constructive feedback. Thank you.

>TOURIST

METRIC CONVERSIONS

TEMPERATURE

- 110° F — 40° C
- 100° F
- 90° F — 30° C
- 80° F
- 70° F — 20° C
- 60° F
- 50° F — 10° C
- 40° F
- 32° F — 0° C
- 20° F
- 10° F — -10° C
- 0° F
- -10° F — -18° C
- -20° F — -30° C

To convert F to C:

Subtract 32, and then multiply by 5/9 or .5555.

To Convert C to F:
Multiply by 1.8 and then add 32.

32F = 0C

LIQUID VOLUME

To Convert:...................Multiply by
U.S. Gallons to Liters................. 3.8
U.S. Liters to Gallons 26
Imperial Gallons to U.S. Gallons 1.2
Imperial Gallons to Liters....... 4.55
Liters to Imperial Gallons 22

1 Liter = .26 U.S. Gallon
1 U.S. Gallon = 3.8 Liters

DISTANCE

To convert ....Multiply by
Inches to Centimeters 2.54
Centimeters to Inches 39
Feet to Meters...................... .3
Meters to Feet 3.28
Yards to Meters 91
Meters to Yards 1.09
Miles to Kilometers 1.61
Kilometers to Miles............ .62

1 Mile = 1.6 km
1 km = .62 Miles

WEIGHT

1 Ounce = .28 Grams
1 Pound = .4555 Kilograms
1 Gram = .04 Ounce
1 Kilogram = 2.2 Pounds

\>TOURIST

TRAVEL QUESTIONS

- Do you bring presents home to family or friends after a vacation?
- Do you get motion sick?
- Do you have a favorite billboard?
- Do you know what to do if there is a flat tire?
- Do you like a sun roof open?
- Do you like to eat in the car?
- Do you like to wear sun glasses in the car?
- Do you like toppings on your ice cream?
- Do you use public bathrooms?
- Did you bring your cell phone and does it have power?
- Do you have a form of identification with you?
- Have you ever been pulled over by a cop?
- Have you ever given money to a stranger on a road trip?
- Have you ever taken a road trip with animals?
- Have you ever went on a vacation alone?
- Have you ever run out of gas?

- If you could move to any place in the world, where would it be?

- If you could travel anywhere in the world, where would you travel?

- If you could travel in any vehicle, which one would it be?

- If you had three things to wish for from a magic genie, what would they be?

- If you have a driver's license, how many times did it take you to pass the test?

- What are you the most afraid of on vacation?

- What do you want to get away from the most when you are on vacation?

- What foods smells bad to you?

- What item to you bring on ever trip with you away from home?

- What makes you sleepy?

- What song would you love to hear on the radio when you're cruising on the highway?

- What travel job would you want the least?

- What will you miss most while you are away from home?

- What is something you always wanted to try?

>TOURIST

- What is the best road side attraction that you ever saw?
- What is the farthest distance you ever biked?
- What is the farthest distance you ever walked?
- What is the weirdest thing you needed to buy while on vacation?
- What is your favorite candy?
- What is your favorite color car?
- What is your favorite family vacation?
- What is your favorite food in the world?
- What is your favorite gas station drink or food?
- What is your favorite license plate design?
- What is your favorite restaurant in the world?
- What is your favorite smell?
- What is your favorite song?
- What is your favorite sound that nature makes?
- What is your favorite thing to bring home from a vacation?
- What is your favorite vacation with friends?
- What is your favorite way to relax?

- What is your favorite weather conditions while driving?
- Where in the world would you rather never get to travel?
- Where is the farthest place you ever traveled in a car?
- Where is the farthest place you ever went North, South, East and West?
- Where is your favorite place in the world?
- Who is your favorite singer?
- Who taught you how to drive?
- Who will you miss the most while you are away?
- Who if the first person you will call when you get to your destination?
- Who brought you on your first vacation?
- Who likes to travel the most in your life?
- Would you rather be hot or cold?
- Would you rather drive above, below, or at the speed limited?
- Would you rather drive on a highway or a back road?
- Would you rather go on a train or a boat?
- Would you rather go to the beach or the woods?

>TOURIST

TRAVEL BUCKET LIST

1.

2.

3.

4.

5.

6.

7.

8.

9.

10.

>TOURIST

NOTES

Made in the USA
Coppell, TX
08 March 2023